THE COTSWOLDS

Paul Felix

ALAN SUTTON

First published in the United Kingdom in 1991 by
Alan Sutton Publishing, Phoenix Mill, Far Thrupp, Stroud,
Gloucestershire

British Library Cataloguing in Publication Data applied for

Typesetting and origination by
Alan Sutton Publishing Limited.
Printed in Great Britain by
The Guernsey Press Company Limited,
Guernsey, The Channel Islands.

THE COTSWOLDS

A land of infinite variety, from the honey-gold stone of the northern
wolds where sheep graze as they have done for centuries, to the
secret valleys of the south with their rushing streams, where the
stone changes to grey and the landscape meets the Severn Vale.

   Throughout the Cotswolds you will find friendly, welcoming
people, happy in their own delightful land but equally glad to share
it with those who come to visit all the year round.

ABLINGTON

Snowdrops carpet the ground outside the quaintly named John Brown's Cottage, not far from the popular village of Bibury.

ANDOVERSFORD

The annual spring sale of horses, one of the most popular of its kind, attracts buyers from a large area. Until recently it was held in Stow-on-the-Wold as part of the town's twice-yearly charter fair, but now takes place at Andoversford.

BADMINTON

Each spring crowds are drawn to one of the premier equestrian events, the Three Day Event held in the grounds of Badminton House.

BADMINTON

Worcester Lodge, on the edge of the Duke of Beaufort's estate, on a sunny winter's morning after a fall of snow.

BAGENDON

A sunny summer's day in the Cotswolds, looking across to the hamlet with its fine old church and eighteenth-century manor-house.

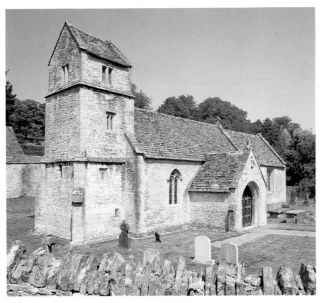

BAGENDON

The church of St Margaret with its saddle-back tower.

BARNSLEY

The house and one of the many colourful borders in Rosemary Verey's prize-winning garden near Cirencester. It is well-known that the Prince of Wales asks Mrs Verey for advice on his own Gloucestershire garden.

BARRINGTON

A game of cricket being played on a summer afternoon with the fine Cotswold house of Barrington Park in the background.

*B*ATH

A quiet corner of the Baths
in this famous Roman city
in the southern Cotswolds,
which is visited by
thousands every year.

*B*AUNTON

The wild flowers add colour
nestling alongside the stone
wall at the edge of a field of
young corn, just outside the
village.

BERKELEY

The cannons stand guard by the gatehouse of this famous castle on the banks of the River Severn. The castle has belonged to the Berkeley family since the Norman Conquest in 1066.

BIBURY

The evening sun rests on Arlington Row which was once weavers' cottages. William Morris is said to have called Bibury 'the prettiest village in England'.

BISLEY

The parish church of Holy Trinity looks out over the Cotswold roofs of the village on a perfect summer's day.

BLOCKLEY

One of the many attractive Cotwold villages on a bright winter's day.

BOURTON-ON-THE-WATER

A summer's day by the River Windrush as it flows beneath one of the famous bridges. They are the reason why Bourton is sometimes called 'the Venice of the Cotswolds'.

BOURTON-ON-THE-WATER

The Cotswolds in miniature can be found in the garden of the Old New Inn where visitors come to look at the scaled-down model of this popular village.

BURFORD

The High Street where the crowds enjoy shopping in the sunshine.

BURFORD

A view of the steep main street and beyond on an early spring day.

CHELTENHAM

The fine gardens along the Promenade in this elegant town, deservedly christened the 'Queen of the Cotswolds'. Once famous for its spa, Cheltenham is now a fashionable shopping centre for the area.

CHELTENHAM

The bandstand next to the Pittville Pump Room. The Pump Room is now one of the few places where it is possible to sample the once celebrated 'Cheltenham waters'.

CHELTENHAM

Far from being a natural landmark, the Devil's Chimney, which overlooks the spa town of Cheltenham, is a strangely shaped column of stone left by Victorian quarrymen.

CHELTENHAM

Snow covers the grounds of Cheltenham College, one of the several public schools built in the last century, for which the town is well known.

CHIPPING CAMPDEN

A late summer afternoon in one of the Cotswolds' most charming towns. Here the historic buildings in the main street are seen through the arches of the seventeenth-century Market House.

CHIPPING CAMPDEN

The Jacobean lodge and gateway are almost all that remains of old Campden Manor which was burned down during the Civil War. To the left is the church of St James's, particularly noted for its fine brasses commemorating famous wool merchants from the town.

CIRENCESTER

St John the Baptist, a church so fine and so large that it is often mistaken for a cathedral by visitors.

CIRENCESTER

The Roman amphitheatre is one of the many reminders of the town's ancient past. In Roman times this was the second largest town in Britain after London.

COMPTON ABDALE

The parish church on a fine spring day.

DAGLINGWORTH

Sheep doze the afternoon away near Cirencester Park, beneath a warm autumn sun.

DONNINGTON

The frozen water mill on this sunny, but cold, day is the small, privately owned brewery near Stow-on-the-Wold.

DUNTISBOURNE ROUSE

The village boasts this beautiful Norman church which attracts visitors from around the world.

Dursley

The parish church of
St James's viewed through
an archway of the
eighteenth-century Market
House where the town
market is still held
twice a week.

Eastington

A barn which typifies the
Cotswold's farming past.
Many such buildings have
been converted into homes
but this one near Northleach
is still used for farming.

EASTLEACH

One of the most picturesque places in the Cotswolds in spring is this riverside village where visitors flock to see the carpets of daffodils.

ELKSTONE

Flowers bloom in profusion in this cottage garden at one of the highest points in the Cotswolds.

FAIRFORD

One of the fine 'wool' churches, so much a part of the history of the Cotswolds, St Mary's in the market town of Fairford is well worth visiting to see its stained glass.

FAIRFORD

An unusual grave in the churchyard marks the resting place of Tibbles the church cat, who kept the church free of mice for many a year.

GLOUCESTER

Reflections of sailing boats
in the recently refurbished
docks, once the site for the
filming of many television
programmes including
The Onedin Line.

GLOUCESTER

The nave of this magnificent
cathedral on a sunny
winter's day.

GREAT TEW

With its delightful thatched cottages this popular village attracts thousands of visitors each year.

GUITING POWER

The war memorial on the village green. This very pretty village with its honey-coloured stone buildings is typical of the northern Cotswolds.

HAILES ABBEY

The ruins of Hailes Abbey near Winchcombe. The abbey was once a favourite retreat for pilgrims before the Dissolution of the Monasteries by Henry VIII.

HIDCOTE

One of Britain's most delightful gardens at Hidcote Manor in the north Cotswolds.

LECHLADE

Halfpenny Bridge, with its
tiny toll-house, arching over
the River Thames.

LECHLADE

The parish church of
St Lawrence standing in a
leafy churchyard which
contains some very elaborate
graves.

LECHLADE

The highest navigable point of the River Thames with St Lawrence's spire in the background.

LECHLADE

The Old Vicarage in the Market Place on a spring day.

LITTLE BARRINGTON

The peace of a winter's day passes undisturbed. During the summer many visitors come to walk around the hamlet with its common and traditional cottages built from locally quarried stone.

LOWER SLAUGHTER

Even in the reflection in the clear waters of the river, the nineteenth-century brick mill contrasts sharply with the traditional Cotswold-stone houses of the village.

MALMESBURY

Malmesbury Abbey with its
magnificent Norman porch.

MICKLETON

Another Cotswold church
bearing the name of
St Lawrence and boasting a
collection of ornate
gravestones.

MORETON-IN-MARSH

The Old Parsonage which
stands near the High Street
of this old market town.

MORETON-IN-MARSH

The Curfew Tower,
probably the town's oldest
building, on a clear winter's
day.

MORETON-IN-MARSH

The early flowers herald the
arrival of spring in Main
Street.

MORETON-IN-MARSH

A sign, dated August 5th
1905, lists the market tolls.
It can be found on the side
of the Curfew Tower.

NAILSWORTH

The south Cotswold
town viewed from
Minchinhampton Common.

NAUNTON

The old dovecote on an
early summer's day, with
marsh marigolds in bloom
beside the stream.

NAUNTON

The sun lights up the
Cotswold stone of the
houses set in the valley of
the River Windrush, near
Stow-on-the-Wold.

NAUNTON

The parish church of
St Andrew in the summer
sunshine.

NORTH CERNEY

A pale spring sun breaks through the mist over the River Churn as it flows through ancient water-meadows.

NORTH CERNEY

The picturesque old church of All Saints, with its saddleback tower, has many fine tombstones in its churchyard which is kept tidy in summer by a flock of local sheep.

NORTH NIBLEY

A monument to William Tyndale, who was burned at the stake for translating the Bible into English, stands high above the Gloucestershire countryside, overlooking the village of North Nibley.

NORTHLEACH

The A40 used to keep this small town choked with traffic. Since a bypass has been built events like the annual steam fair are enjoyed without the roar of traffic competing against the steam engines.

OZLEWORTH

Sheep graze on a November
day on a hillside at
Ozleworth Park near the
south Cotswold town of
Wotton-Under-Edge, once
well known for its
production of fine woollen
cloth.

PAINSWICK

The elegant spire of
St Mary's Church towers
above the famous
churchyard with its
eighteenth-century table-top
tombs and ninety-nine
clipped yews. Legend has it
that the hundredth yew will
never grow.

RENDCOMB

A misty early morning dawns on a winter's day, as the sun lights up the village and the well-known college built early this century by a local benefactor.

RODMARTON

This fine herbaceous border is at Rodmarton Manor, near Cirencester. The house in the background was completed in the late 1920s, the last manor-house to be built in England.

ROLLRIGHTS

The King's Men Stones with
an artist at work painting
the legendary landmarks.

SELSLEY

The water garden at Selsley
Herb Farm, near Stroud, on
a sunny summer's day.
Once a farmyard, the garden
now attracts visitors from all
over the world.

SNOWSHILL

Snowshill, set high in the
Cotswolds near the popular
centre of Broadway, is an
appropriate setting for a
winter's scene. The village
and manor-house attract
many visitors on warmer
days.

SNOWSHILL

Snowshill Manor boasts a
variety of extraordinary
objects, including these
figures of St George and the
dragon.

STOW-ON-THE-WOLD

The old stocks are just one point of interest in this historic market town with its narrow streets, its ancient charter and its associations with the Civil War.

STOW-ON-THE-WOLD

Gypsy horses tied to the railings of a pub during the Stow horse fair. A fair has been held here twice a year by Royal Charter for hundreds of years.

STROUD

A beautiful November day
at Stratford Park.

STROUD

A pen and her cygnets enjoy
a fine day on the
Thames and Severn Canal
near Stroud.

SWINBROOK

The church of St Mary in this Oxfordshire village photographed late in the summer.

TETBURY

This disused road is next to the old toll-house on the edge of this attractive town. In the background is the elegant spire of the parish church of St Mary.

TETBURY

A spot known as 'The Chipping Steps'.

TEWKESBURY

The magnificent Abbey Church of St Mary reflected in the flood waters near where the Rivers Severn and Avon meet.

TUNLEY

An idyllic Cotswold cottage set in a pretty garden in this quiet backwater, a few miles from Cirencester.

UPPER SLAUGHTER

Early morning in this picturesque village high on the Cotswolds before the visitors arrive to share its joys.

UPTON ST LEONARDS

The modern building of
Prinknash Abbey attracts
many visitors to see the
monks at work in the
famous pottery.

WESTONBIRT

The arboretum near Tetbury
is popular with visitors
throughout the year but
particularly in the autumn
when the colours are
absolutely breathtaking.

WESTWELL

A visitor studies the Norman church in this Oxfordshire village.

WESTWELL

The old Post Office set in this pretty hamlet near Burford. The village is missed by many but it is certainly worth a detour to see the fine buildings clustered around the village pond.

WINCHCOMBE

The Gloucestershire Morris Men dance in the town centre on a spring day. There has been a significant revival of the old country customs in the Cotswolds in recent years.

WINCHCOMBE

One of the fine gargoyles on St Peter's Church.

WINSON

A quiet corner of the Coln Valley on a sunny summer's day. The thatched roof on this little summerhouse is something of a rarity in the Cotswolds.

WOODCHESTER

The building of this seemingly magnificent mansion in Woodchester Park near Stroud began in 1846. A few years later work mysteriously stopped and the house has never been finished.

WOTTON-UNDER-EDGE

A pale winter sun lights the
Cotswold stone on the
fine parish church of
St Mary the Virgin in this
former cloth-making town.

WOTTON-UNDER-EDGE

The clock on the Tolsey
House.

YANWORTH

On a misty November day
the early morning sun
illuminates this scene just
outside the village of
Yanworth in the mid-
Cotswolds.